AF472165

HITLER

(A View of the 1935 Reichsparteitag By a Member of the Académie Française)

By

Louis Bertrand,
Translation by Dan Desjardins

1663 Liberty Drive, Suite 200
Bloomington, Indiana 47403
(800) 839-8640
www.AuthorHouse.com

First published by AuthorHouse 10/25/05

ISBN: 1-4208-6801-2 (sc)

Library of Congress Control Number: 2005905848

Printed in the United States of America
Bloomington, Indiana

This book is printed on acid-free paper.

Cover photo courtesy D.D. Desjardins from collection formerly held at U.S. Army Pueblo Chemical Depot, Pueblo CO. By permission Public Affairs, HQ Chemical Materials Agency, Aberdeen MD.

Table of Contents

Translator's Introduction

The following text by Louis Bertrand has remained, understandably, a work quite remote to most Anglophone readers, though I dare say this is true even for most Frenchmen as well. Indeed, my first inquiry to the original publisher, Arthème Fayard, brought the response that Monsieur Bertrand, holder of a chair at the prestigious Sorbonne, prominent scholar, author of great books on subjects such as Louis XIV, Saint Augustine, and Saint Teresa, would not likely have condescended to write on such a vulgar person as "le Führer." And yet the evidence was there, not only from the pen of Kurt G. W. Ludecke, who first revealed the fact for me in his own book "I Knew Hitler" (Jarrolds Publishers, London, 1938) but by virtue of actually acquiring the quaint-looking text through inter-library loan from the University of North Carolina, Chapel Hill. Arthème Fayard did acknowledge Louis Bertrand's authorship, as well as the fact of their publication, some ten years later when I sent a photocopy of the original title page.

From the Dictionary of French Biography, Volume 6, we learn that Monsieur Bertrand was born at Spincourt, March 20, 1866. He studied at Bar-le-Duc, went on to complete his university studies and upon graduation at age 22, became a grammar-school teacher in Aix-La-Provence. Three years later, he moved to Bourg-en-Bresse, seeking refuge from public condemnation over an eulogy he made concerning Emile Zola.[1] In 1891 Monsieur Bertrand obtained a chair in Algeria, a beginning that would influence much of his later life. He received a Doctor of Letters in 1897 with the thesis, "The End of Classicism and the Return to Antiquity In the Second Half of the 18th Century and First Years of the 19th Century in France," followed in 1899 by his first book, "The Blood of the Races," which dealt with heredity and the crossing of racial groups in Algeria. Bertrand's first novels appeared shortly thereafter, including "Don Juan's Rival" (1903) and "Pépète and Balthazar." In 1906 Monsieur Bertrand traveled to the Orient, where he became passionately interested in questions of religion. After several accounts and novels based on his travels, including "Greece of Sun and Countryside" (1908) and "Mademoiselle from Jessincourt" (1911), he published "Saint Augustine" (1913), the first of his religious studies and one whose renown immediately classed him among the masters of artistic hagiography. "Sanguis Martyrum" appeared

[1] Emile Zola, 1840-1902: whose major work was the "Rougon-Macquart" series, 20 novels (1871-1893), portraying the recurrence and development of transmitted characteristics over five generations in one family. He was one of the leaders of the Naturalist literary movement.

toward the end of World War I, a book in which Bertrand extolled the virtues of heroism to his fellow Frenchmen. “Louis XIV” appeared in 1923, followed by “Jean Perbal” in 1925. In this same year, Monsieur Bertrand was elected to the prestigious Académie Française, an honor bestowed to France’s most deserving academicians. In 1924 he again pursued a religious theme with the publication of “Saint Teresa,” a personage for whom he had great admiration. “The New Sentimental Education” and “Hippolyte Porte-Couronnes” appeared in 1932. His later years were devoted to history: “History of Spain,” and works on Lorraine and Africa among these. His memoirs were contained in a series of novels under the title “d’Une Destinée,” of which 8 volumes appeared, to be followed by others, when he died on December 6, 1941, at Cap d’Antibes, North Africa.

A note concerning the present translation. In every instance, I have attempted to render the most exact meaning to the author’s words. However, given there is always some measure of choice as to how to turn a phrase, I have also attempted to produce an English translation that is structurally and aesthetically pleasing. The French construct, if used per its original form, would on numerous occasions have produced rather awkward results. A few examples serve to illustrate. On page 70 of the original text, Louis Bertrand writes:

> “L’idéal lointain, c’est de refaire cette armée, de resserrer la centralisation dans les cadres

administratifs, c'est enfin de réduire le parlement à son rôle, consultatif…"

Literally translated, this would read:

> The remote ideal, it is to remake this army, to retighten the centralization in the administrative echelons, it is finally to reduce the parliament to its consultative role.

Instead I have rendered the above to read:

> The eventual goal was* to rebuild this army, to solidify centralized authority through administrative echelons, and ultimately to reduce parliament to its consultative role…

(* context within the actual paragraph further makes clear the tense requires verb conjugation into the imperfect rather than the present)

Or again on page 75 of Bertrand's text:

> "Avec les manifestations et les réunions, la propagande par l'affiliation et surtout par la press."

Again, the literal translation would appear quite awkward, since Bertrand's phrasing is a sentence structure without verb:

> “With demonstrations and meetings, propaganda by association and above all by the press.”[2]

Here I have made the translation more palatable by rendering a complete sentence:

> “In the wake of their demonstrations and gatherings, the National Socialists gained publicity by word of mouth, and above all, through the press.”

Another point concerns tense. Monsieur Bertrand, narrating events of the recent past, including those he personally witnessed, wrote in the present tense. The impression this gives, when reading now, is rather awkward. We have, for example, on page 74:

> “En 1922, à Koburg, il organise une <<Journée allemande>>.” (In 1922, at Coburg, he organizes a “German Day.”)

For stylistic purposes, as well as a more comfortable temporal sense, I have deemed it appropriate to re-conjugate Bertrand’s verbs into the past tense. Hence, with the above example, one will find:

> “In 1922, in the city of Coburg, Hitler arranged to celebrate ‘German Day’.”

---

2 Translator’s Note: I suspect Bertrand’s draft to Arthème Fayard came in the form of diary entries.

Despite such deviations as mentioned above, I have nevertheless attempted to preserve a correct interpretation of Louis Bertrand's observations and expression. Any aberration in this regard is wholly unintentional, for which I take full responsibility.

Louis Bertrand. Courtesy Bettmann Archive.

Author's Forward

For a long time now, we French have behaved in an unreasonable manner on the subject of Hitler and Hitlerism. And, although for the moment we are experiencing a mild détent, not so much in regard to Hitler as in regard to the German nation, we continue to be unreasonable about him as about Germany herself.

We began by not taking him seriously, then by declaring he would not last very long. We even tried to ridicule him as we had done with Mussolini. We called him "house painter," just like we had called the other "carnival Caesar." However, this "painter of houses" has not only created a revolution, but he has restored to Germany her military force and prestige as a great nation. He has torn up the treaties that pretended to reduce her to a state of perpetual inferiority, if not slavery. He has reconquered her liberty! And not only does he endure, but promises to do so for a long time to come! But instead of viewing these facts with the attention and intelligence they merit, we prefer to jest, and because we can do nothing about his persistence, hope for his downfall, persuading ourselves it is inevitable! We are doing everything we can to bring this about, not by energetic action, but by gossip and idle considerations.

We are like the Athenians in decline, who, when confronted with the warlike preparations of Philip, confined themselves to repeating hearsay tales such as: "he is ill" or, "he is dead!" or, "he is going to die!" Demosthenes made sport of these brave patriots who relied only upon a bad cold or a poisoner's potient by which to rid themselves of their enemy. We have come to this point ourselves! We gleefully welcome the tittle-tattle of those who assure us the finances of the Reich are at the point of bankruptcy, when indeed, they are no worse than our own, which are on the brink of devaluation. We are told the Germans have no more butter, no more sausage, no more pork, nor meat, and that, doubtless, they will soon be out of bread. Indeed, they prefer to forego these things for guns. In any event they are not, as are we, people who eat bread. We are still being told that the Catholic and Christian conscience is in rebellion against the ideology and tendencies of the regime, and that this can only favor the disaffection of the masses, already deceived in all their hopes and material desires. In the meantime, those who believe this are doing nothing, regardless whether certain pastors or bishops give the appearance of protest. And the churches and temples themselves continue to behave as if nothing was wrong.

To what purpose does it serve to stir up ideas of this sort and to feed us with illusions and hopes too likely disappointed? Nevertheless, these are the ideas and illusions I recently found in a rather gloomy article in "La Revue des Deux Mondes."[1] The author is himself so uncertain the lack of butter and revolt of Christian conscience are premonitory symptoms of coming catastrophe that he is careful to tell us the ultimate downfall is not for tomorrow. "It will require some time," he concedes, "for the hate to become revolt." But first of all, what do you really know about this? The worse thing in the world is to divert French opinion away from considerations of the present toward a future which is even more uncertain. This tends to nurture dangerous illusions in persons already too willing to believe the adversary is on his last legs. What is important for us to see isn't Germany in revolt tomorrow - if ever she will be - but a Germany today which is disciplined and obedient. The most dangerous consideration is less what is said than what is implied: the belief that once Hitler is deposed, things will go better for us and for peace in Europe. However, it is difficult to see what we might gain from a Germany in the hands of the Junkers or a Germany controlled by the Bolshevists. For we can hardly anticipate but these two alternatives. And for our eastern neighbors, the most likely would be the advent of Bolshevism. God forbid!

---

[1] "Le mécontment allemand" ("the German Dissatisfaction"), by Robert d'Harcourt, 15 December 1935.

Concerning the vast majority of Frenchmen, something even more disheartening is the persistence of backwardness, of political fossilism, that consists in believing we can prevent the Germans from having a government according to their own taste, and finally, that we can organize a new Europe, or simply our own security, without or against Germany. All these errors proceed from a presumptuous ignorance, not only about Germany, but about modern Europe and the world in general: an ignorance carefully maintained by an idiotic and mercenary press. Its efforts ignominiously deceive the nation, the resultant ignorance revealing itself either as a lack of awareness or a scandalous imprudence by those among us who are the least pardonable: our politicians and our leaders. It is in this way that the last war was concocted and served to the nation, imposed as an inevitable necessity, by people who did nothing to avoid it, and still less to prepare for it. Both leaders and followers were brutally placed before the accomplished fact, willed there by the whims of the occult. They marched there blindly, after trying to negotiate when it was too late. A succession of errors committed in ignorance and darkness brought us to this catastrophe. Here is where a foreign policy abandoned to misinformed parliamentarians leads, men numbed by the worry of re-election and unable to see anything beyond the borders of their own precinct.

Frenchmen in general knew nothing of the underpinnings of that war, which fell upon them like a meteorite, and which they were subjected to without being asked. To fully appreciate France's unawareness and lack of knowledge, it is necessary to read the memoirs of our leaders at that time: the admission of their bewilderment and powerlessness is, for a patriotic Frenchman, something profoundly humiliating and painful.

Just as France knew nothing of the underpinnings for this war, she also knew nothing about what was going on behind-the-scenes during the war's aftermath. After preparing her for a horrible and absurd war, she was then served an equally absurd and disastrous peace. And this peace was secured in the same ignorance and unawareness to which the nation was subjected as a whole, with the addition of the most juvenile illusions thrown in for good measure. Let us recall our state of mind following the armistice of 1918. We had just lived through four years of suffering and anguish, having experienced the worst dangers in France's history. Two months earlier, we had come within inches of being finally and definitively beaten.[1] And then, suddenly, with the relief of the Americans, our peril disappeared and victory once again appeared on

[1] Translator's Note: the truth of this notwithstanding, Marshal Foch gave a rare press interview in Trier to members of General Pershing's press corps, 17 January 1919, where he was asked what would have happened had the Germans not sued for peace on 11 November 1918. Marshal Foch, in the company of AEF Commander General Pershing, outlined plans for "The Battle of Lorraine," scheduled to be launched 14 November. This battle would have entailed the armies of France and the United States enveloping Germany in a giant pincer movement, ending with the capture of Berlin (see George Seldes, Witness to a Century, Ballantine Books, New York, N.Y., 1987, p. 110).

the horizon. We were delirious! The Germanic terror was no longer but a bad dream. This Germany which had almost planted its foot on our neck, which had covered our land with ruins and hideous carnage, was finished at last! We persuaded ourselves that, thanks to our second retaking of the Marne, thanks to our allies, and thanks finally to the Treaty of Versailles, not only had all danger been averted, but there was no longer any Germany left to reckon with. After all, wasn't she reduced to impotence, to famine, and impoverishment? Hadn't she been crushed by obligations to pay billions of marks in reparations, forced to submit to the presence of occupation troops who held her at their mercy, reduced by the military clauses of the treaty to a state of inferiority, if not perpetual weakness? The administrators who, by supreme blunder, were mostly Frenchmen, were supposed to oversee the full execution of these clauses. Declared responsible for the war, Germany was placed in the penitence dock of Europe, if not the entire world. For the first time, a moral stigma intervened in a treaty of peace.

It is very important to recognize: never has a defeated nation been subjected to similar treatment. The victors imposed restrictions to the point of making it nearly impossible for Germany to recuperate. But we should also recognize that if the Germans had been the victors, they would certainly have imposed similar or even worse conditions on us.[2] The fact is, however, they

---

[2] Translator's Note: although it is understandable for Monsieur Bertrand to believe this, in point of fact, Hitler was quite lenient after the fall of France in June, 1940. For example, southern

were not the victors, and therefore it was not they who did this. It was we and our allies who imposed these conditions, without parallel in history, except perhaps in the time of Sennacherib and Tamerlane.[3] From the perspective of justice and reason, we must condemn these collective subjugations of an entire people, race, and civilization: it is a good idea to bring this to mind, especially for the Germans, who already have too great a tendency towards these brutal and summary methods. All the while, however, under certain circumstances, I admit the necessities of war and the law of might. We might have been able to impose these harsh intentions on our enemy had we actually been the stronger adversary, but in reality we were not. We needed our allies to insure adequate respect for these conditions. And these allies, whose interests were very different from our own, were in no way intending to support our pretensions. They instead put us in a quandary. We were left on our own before a Germany whose immediate and central desire was revenge.

Matters being such, we had two courses to decide between: either maintain ourselves on an intensive war

---

France, with its new seat of government at Vichy, remained unoccupied, while the bulk of the French Navy was allowed to remain unmolested at Toulon.

[3] Translator's Note: Sennacherib: King of Assyria 705 - 681 B.C., son and successor to Sargon II, who, because of his attack on Jerusalem, figured prominently in the Old Testament; also in Lord Byron's "The Destruction of Sennacherib"; Tamerlane: (Timur Lenk) 1336 - 1405, Turkish warrior, noted for conquests from Hormuz, on the Indian coast, to Chistopol, on the Volga, as well as for an attempted invasion of China in 1404.

footing, or reconcile ourselves, according to mutual interests, with our recent enemy (and no doubt, we had the advantage!). But we did neither. Instead, we alternately inflicted the Germans with unnecessary and dangerous humiliations, such as the Ruhr occupation (according to the plan of Poincaré[4]), and we granted them useless and haphazard concessions (stemming from the plan of Briand[5]). Humiliations and concessions lead in sum to the same result: they exasperated German feelings against us by keeping the Germans in a perpetual state of inferiority. We did this by exercising a pretension we would not abandon, we, the weaker of the two parties. And for all the concessions to which we consented, the essential clause of what the Germans called the "diktat" of Versailles was left in place: to whit, the prohibition against re-armament beyond a given level.

Instead, Germany began arming herself right under our very nose while we wasted our time in juridical chicaneries, grudgingly giving concessions always considered insufficient, while offering everyone and

---

[4] Translator's Note: Raymond Poincaré (1860-1934), President of the French Republic during World War I, who, as Prime Minister and Minister for Foreign Affairs (1922-1924), ordered the French occupation of the Ruhr in 1923 in response to Germany's default on reparations payments.

[5] Translator's Note: Aristide Briand (1862-1932), French Foreign Minister co-responsible for the 1925 Locarno Pact that attempted to normalize relations between Germany and her former enemies. Briand was an early advocate for a federal union of Europe.

their brother vagabond security agreements just as ridiculous as they were onerous and ineffectual.

In order to be steadfast, one must be strong. And it is necessary to be strong even if only to create a proper respect for one's treaties. Nevertheless, it has become a cliché of popular controversy to reproach our government for the evacuation of the Rhine and the abandonment of Mainz.[2] Could it have been otherwise? During the time of the Ruhr episode, I heard a Marshal of France declare: "Our Army is reduced to a mere skeleton!" In order to hold the bridgeheads of the enemy, it appears necessary to have strong contingents ready to go into action at the first alert. Was this the case with us? Towards the end of 1934, I participated in a rather agitated demonstration at the Sorbonne regarding the Sarre question. The result of this demonstration was to demand we should go to war. Were we ready?

There are those who believe we could have achieved our ends by bringing Germany back to the status of individual states, even more completely and definitively than in the Middle Ages under the Holy Roman Empire or the hegemony of Prussia. These are the illusions of Chartists[6] or former nationalists, who think it still possible, in this day and age, to return to

---

[2] Translator's Note: Mainz to the French is known as Mayence. Ceded to France by the Treaty of Campo Formio in 1797, restored to Germany in 1814. After W.W. I it was occupied by Allied troops.

[6] Translator's Note: Chartism: An English political movement begun in 1838 based on the "People's Charter," embodying

what existed with great difficulty during the reign of Louis XIV and Napoleon: the division of the various German states, an independent Bavaria, an autonomous Rhineland (or one re-attached to France)… Yes, perhaps if our allies had stood by us. But England had no interest in delivering us from a rival who consumed, to the point of exhaustion, our nearly every effort and action.

In order to keep us preoccupied, to weaken and render us relatively harmless toward others, it was necessary that a unified Germany exist in our presence as a continual threat.

Let us suppose, however, that our allies allowed us a free hand regarding our vanquished enemy; that they even helped us divide Germany and keep her under control: does anyone believe this charming accomplishment would last for very long? It is not necessary to know Germany in order to realize that a nation of 65 million people, conscious of the value of a united empire in terms of power and prestige, would never be able to resign themselves to a division which brought about a perpetual state of weakness and inferiority.

---

six points: universal manhood suffrage, vote by secret ballot, annually elected Parliaments, equal population electoral districts, payment of members of Parliament, and abolition of property requirement for members of Parliament. The charter was repeatedly rejected by the House of Commons, up to and including its final rejection in 1848. Since that time, five of its six points were eventually put into practice, the exception being annual election of members of Parliament.

But what is the use of reasoning over what is not, and cannot be! The incontestable fact at the present time is that our momentary victory can, from one day to the next, be put back in question. We are facing a Germany more unified and more centralized than ever before, a nation that has once again become a military power of first magnitude.

The current German Chancellor, Adolf Hitler, has put his personal stamp on the work of recovery. What his actual part is in this giant collective movement towards recovery is difficult to tell. But it is certain the result is due, in a significant way, to his personal influence and the effect he has on the masses.

Hitler is roundly detested by a large number of Frenchmen who consider him a monster and reproach him for a great number of villainous things, notably his perfidy, his inconstancy toward treaties, and his rearmament in contradiction to declarations of peace.

It is up to the moralists to judge Man and his conduct. We are concerned here only with political considerations, painfully aware that politics and morality, in reality, are often strangers to one another. So be it. It is necessary to resign oneself to the inevitable here, holding fast, nevertheless, to individual and international moral principles. Louis XIV, who had no illusions in this regard, instructed his eldest son: "In adapting oneself to the observance of treaties, you can never be accused of infringement, because the words are never taken to the letter, since these were the only ones that could be employed." Isn't it a rather childish naïveté to reproach Hitler for tearing up the military stipulations of the Versailles Treaty, once he was able to do so with impunity? Since when is a treaty respected that one was forced to sign with a knife at one's throat? Regarding ourselves, didn't we tear up the Treaty of Frankfurt once we were able, by force of arms?[3]

Above all, we reproach Hitler for certain passages in *Mein Kampf* directed against our country. He has subsequently dismissed these remarks, although we are told they have not been removed from the new editions of his book. We forget, or at least pretend to forget, that this book is 15 years old, written at a time when Germany might have correctly considered France its greatest enemy. Circumstances have changed since then and they can indeed change once more: something that might explain Hitler's attitude in regard to our country. By now offering us a pact of mutual cooperation, there is no reason not to consider him as sincere in 1936 as he was in 1921, when speaking about a settling of accounts. In politics, especially with the Germans, we must accustom ourselves to successive sincerities, dictated by events and changing situations, never more

---

[3] Translator's Note: the Treaty of Frankfurt was negotiated for the French by Adolphe Thiers, and ratified by the French National Assembly on 1 March 1871. The treaty, which ended the Franco-Prussian War, obliged France to provide Germany 5 billion francs in reparations, plus the cost of maintaining a German occupation army in eastern France and the annexation of Alsace and half of Lorraine.

unstable than at this moment. It is contrary to the spirit of trust to confront Hitler with phrases written so long ago, that he now disavows and that can no longer be true anyway, unless they become such through our own fault. For their part, the Germans reproach us with the mischievous conduct of our press, to which we respond with recriminations against theirs. "One cannot trust the Germans!" we say, and yet, all this is very infantile. It is always the gravest imprudence to trust people with whom one is obliged to deal. And through our candor we would like to be sure we will not be tricked by our partner. But in reality, this is too much to ask. When playing this game, we must always expect to be cheated, while doing the impossible so as not to be, especially since we are not at liberty to accept or refuse this game in the first place.

As a final point, it is merely a journalistic argument, a polemical cliché, to deny the Führer's declarations of peace because of Germany's massive and continuous rearmament. It is too easy for him to reply that Germany is surrounded by enemies, given we have done everything to convince him of this fact, not only in attempting to organize the ridiculous Petite-Entente, but in signing a treaty with the Soviets.

I realize that the above discussion could go on indefinitely. For the moment, however, the only thing of importance is for us to see, not necessarily the character of our adversary, but what he means to us, and the actions we take relative to the policies he follows and the plans he allows us to perceive. In other words, faced by Hitlerian Germany, what do we need to do? And, regarding the National Socialist movement, existing and advancing in spite of us, how can we turn it to account for our least harm, or our greatest good?

In the pages that follow, it is not the intent to satisfy the reader's idle curiosity by bringing him unedited details about Hitler's character or private life. Nor is it the intent to say anything about Hitlerism itself or about its German political doctrine. It is not a matter of the one or the other except to the degree it affects we Frenchmen. It is uniquely from a French point of view and with French interests in mind that we will consider the following subjects.

Hitler speaks. Courtesy Library of Congress.

Hitler greets the masses. Courtesy Library of Congress.

Hitler at Nuremberg, flanked by Wilhelm Keitel and Rudolph Hess. Courtesy Library of Congress.

Schutzstaffel in formation. Courtesy Library of Congress.

I

How I Viewed Hitler

For us, the person of Hitler seems enveloped in a cloud; a hero of Germanic or Scandinavian mythology about whom we perceive only the lance, the sword, or the helmet.

The world press has told us a great deal about him, yet his personality remains shrouded by this Nordic mist. His biographies, even his own memoirs, leave us with a rather imprecise physiognomy, an individuality but slightly delineated. In the final analysis, it is not Hitler the individual who interests us, but the work upon which he has put his name, and the great collective force he represents. And yet, we should not be resigned to vagueness or imprecision. We would like to uncover the secret of such prodigious fortune and success.

Let us resume in a broad way what the world knows about him. He is an Austrian, albeit from the Bavarian foothills. He was born on 10 April 1889[1] in Braunau on the banks of the Inn. He accompanied his father, a minor customs official, to Passau and Linz. In sum, his entire childhood and adolescence took place on German soil. What is more, he is a man of the frontier. And, like all those of the frontier, he has a greater sense of race and the enemy than most other Germans.

With strict upbringing and thwarted childhood, Hitler became an orphan at an early age, thereby knowing hardship and even misery. All this has quite an effect in tempering one's ambition. The first signs of a possible vocation were given in regard to drawing and painting. Later, he would persuade himself, or else someone else would persuade him, that his true career resided with architecture. And all this is quite significant and rather startling for a future statesman: this taste for form and structure, this instinct for working with what is real and to shape and construct it. Orphan at the age of 15, he went to Vienna in the hopes of using his talents as designer and watercolorist. He was unsuccessful. Yet, this visit to Vienna exerted a profound influence on the direction of his ideas. He experienced the decline of an empire made of incongruous pieces, where Germanism was menaced by the influx of concurrent races, where the Germans were inundated by a mingling of Czechs, Poles, Hungarians, Ruthenians, Serbians, Croatians, and Jews. The racist that he would become was taking his first lessons. He saw an all powerful Jewry and,

---

[1] Translator's Note: Bertrand is mistaken. The world knows and accepts 20 April 1889 as Adolf Hitler's correct birthdate.

side-by-side with a social democracy manipulated by Jews, he was also witness to the vigorous reactions of Catholic anti-Semitism. Nothing of all this would be lost upon him.

In 1912, Hitler arrived in Munich, not long before the war that was to interrupt his still confused racist and nationalist theories. He enlisted as a volunteer in a Bavarian regiment, was wounded in 1916, at which point he was temporarily blinded. He underwent treatment in a hospital in Pomerainia, during which time the revolution exploded with the signing of the armistice.[2] He cried with shame in the face of such total humiliation. Thereafter, his course was determined. He would go into politics and work for the recovery of Germany. He thus returned to Munich, his point of departure. There, he met Gottfried Feder, theoretician of the "German Workers' Movement," the precursor of National Socialism.[3] He spoke during their meetings, making a very inauspicious beginning: his audience

---

[2] Translator's Note: according to Hitler's own account in "Mein Kampf," his blinding by gas occurred during the British attack at Ypres, 14 October 1918. The armistice came the following month. Incidence of a partial revolt affecting the German Navy occurred as early as 1917, following the Peace Resolution declared by Chancellor Mathias Erzberger's Social Democratic Center Party on 19 July.

[3] Translator's Note: (1883 - 1941), A civil engineer by profession, founder of the German Fighting League for the Breaking of Interest Slavery, and author of "National and Social Bases of the German State" (1923). He became State Secretary of the German Ministry of Economics in 1933 and State Housing Commissioner in 1934.

numbered 20 or 25 persons. But he obtained the habit of oratory, developed himself into a public speaker, and soon became someone who could allure the masses. Yet the crowds still belonged, by and large, to International Marxism. It was therefore necessary to vanquish Marxism in order to bring about the recovery of Germany.

Thus began for Hitler a period of struggle, of brushes with danger at the risk of his life. By 1921, the National Socialist Party had a Program.[4] It was an effort to vanquish as much by persuasion as by violence. Hitler opposed the Marxists with terror for terror. He invaded the adversary's syndicalist bastions and, little by little, having conquered the masses, hoped to succeed by legal means. Massive votes and successful plebiscites gave him confidence. Assisted by every manner of political intrigue, he succeeded in becoming an actual dictator. By 1934, in his role as Führer and Reich Chancellor, he succeeded President Hindenburg. In 1935, Hitler decisively broke with the Treaty of Versailles, and, while rebuilding national unity, reestablished the imperial armed forces. It was more than a mere victory - it was a quintessential glory!

In 15 years the little orphan from Braunau had become the incontestable leader - more absolute than

[4] Translator's Note: in truth, the National Socialist German Workers' Party Program was first presented at the Party's mass-meeting in the Hofbrauhausfestsaal in Munich on 24 February 1920.

the ancient sovereigns of Europe - of a nation of 65 million people: almost the same time it took Bonaparte to gird the imperial crown.

During mid-September of last year, I had an entire week's opportunity to see up close the hero of this extraordinary adventure.[5] It was for the celebration of the Reichsparteitag, or Reich's Party Day, which lasted a full seven days; a unique occasion to view Hitler as the public figure he is, in contact and communion with his people. I didn't want to miss it. Such an event should interest a Frenchman to the highest degree, and particularly a professional observer such as myself. Since it is always easy to deprecate the most laudable intentions, it is necessary for me to say I am not an Hitlerian: an Hitlerian Frenchman seems to me an absurdity. Yet it is necessary to expect all manner of foolishness. I was in Nuremberg for the sole reason to observe and better understand: this is the duty of every patriot capable of exercising any sort of influence on public opinion. I have limited myself to reporting on what I saw and commenting on my impressions.

Most everyone knows that Nuremberg has become a Mecca of sorts for the German National Socialists and that, every year, for an entire week, people from all over Germany go there to celebrate the victory of the Party.

---

[5] Translator's Note: i.e., 1935.

The choice of Nuremberg for this occasion is certainly very fortunate. First of all, it is a city of art and a very beautiful city besides. Nevertheless, I do not share all of the Germans' admiration for it. Though offering some charming areas, notably the wharfs and bridges of the Pegnitz, it does not have any monuments of first order. It is also important to recognize that the abuse of Gothic stylization - all the modern houses are more or less imitations copied from the XV or XVI century - detracts from the authentic edifices and antiquities which do exist. Such as it is, the atmosphere there is certainly more inviting than at Berlin, the general aspect being much more agreeable.

Alongside the ancient city, the Party has built a special city for its own use - a city where everything is of colossal dimensions, with arenas, marching fields, auditoriums for gatherings and conferences, theatre and concerts. Already in existence is the Stadium, the Luitpold Arena, the Luitpold Hall, and Zeppelin Field, while awaiting the Congressional Palace, which is expected to be something magnificent, a project of Romanesque proportions and a masterpiece of Germanic grandeur. The breadth is expected to measure 260 meters. The main hall will provide for 60,000 persons. And next to this gigantic room will be others smaller in size - among these, a thousand-person meeting room, and a concert hall able to accommodate 3,000… everything in proportion.

As we descended from the train, we were given a program of the upcoming festivities that, like the newer Nuremberg, were something tremendous: seven entire days of processions, of military parades, of fanfare, of concerts, of theatrical performances, of torchlight ceremonies. In the midst of all this, a torrent of speeches, including those by the Führer, who was scheduled to speak each day. Throughout the entire city were hung immense red flags, in the center of which the swastika stood out in black on a white background, the ancient colors of the Empire: a symbolic means of associating the present revolution with the former traditions of imperial Germany; an affirmation not to break with the past. And in the buttonhole of their shirt or jacket, everyone wore the Party motif for 1935: an effigy of Hitler flanked by a storm trooper and a steal-helmeted soldier, all crowned by the swastika and the imperial eagle. It is said these two images represent the two pillars of the regime: the political might of the Party and a nation in arms. The whole signifies, it would seem, that "Adolf Hitler is Germany and Germany is Adolf Hitler."[6]

We were assured there would be at least one million two hundred thousand visitors coming around the clock by train to Nuremberg, from all over Germany. What is certain is that during those days I witnessed a virtually uninterrupted military procession: the image of a nation wholly militarized. That raising of shovels, that teeming of bayonets - filled the peaceful streets of the ancient city of the meister-singers; the sound of boots

---

[6] Translator's Note: Louis Bertrand is no doubt recalling the description spoken by Rudolf Hess during his closing speech at the Reichsparteitag ceremonies.

hammering the pavement hour by hour, those men of all ages and demeanor, in battle-dress, equipped and ready for action, in long, interminable close-ranked rows - this was something both bewildering and overwhelming: the mobilization of an entire people!

One could not say these men, who were singing, who wore a flower in their helmet or cap, were particularly joyous. You could sense the fatigue on their faces, almost all of them hard and inexpressive: while watching them, the word "gregarious" naturally comes to the lips of a Frenchman. They did not exactly appear as if they were at a festival. Rather, a rigid discipline was stamped on all their faces, regulating their every movement. Did they actually accept all this discipline, were they full of the "dedication to the Führer and faith in his mission," as the leaders of the Party proclaimed? What I do know is that the enthusiasm of the crowd contrasted strangely with this fierce and silent discipline. And yet, the enthusiasm itself seemed disciplined. Nothing comparable to the crowds in France, where spontaneity of movement and the shout of the individual always manifests itself. This instead was the marvelously regulated activity of a unified body. From the moment the Führer's procession was announced, a human torrent hurried out to meet him. And from this moving sea of people arose cheers and acclamation, propagating itself like a rolling thunder. Here, truly, was an emotion, a heartfelt emotion issuing from all these people. I can honestly say I have never witnessed such delirium. I asked myself what sovereign, what national hero had been acclaimed, adulated, cherished and idolized as much as this man, this diminutive man in brown shirt who, followed by his retinue, like a sovereign, nevertheless had the air of a worker. This was certainly something other than mere popularity: it was religion. Hitler, in the eyes of his admirers, is nothing less than a prophet, a divine oracle. I have received letters from Germany written by ordinary people who exalt him as God's Chosen and a masterpiece of creation…

After viewing the enormity and immeasurable character of that military parade, the magnificence of scenery, the superb artistry used in decoration, and the harmonious flow of all those people, I can say I have never seen anything more beautiful regarding this type of event. Everything had been organized as if it were part of a colossal opera.

The evening of my arrival, I attended a gala presentation of the Meister-Singers at the Nuremberg Grand Theatre. Hitler was in attendance, surrounded by his general staff, while the room was filled with well-known Reich political figures, invited guests and elite members of the general public. There prevailed a grand simplicity in the dress, the uniforms, and even the female attire. Behavior was exemplary, even somewhat contemplative, as if in a church; everything one might imagine in regard to the Land of Wagner. What is more, the impressions of sight and sentiment which I found here, among this chosen public, I again found on a scale infinitely greater - a hundred-fold more impressive - in all the various ceremonies and demonstrations which I attended. The entirety preserved a character of mass appeal, quite befitting the city of shoemaker Hans Sachs. And yet, nevertheless, through its pious patriotism, and the fervor and meditative silence of the people, all this took on a certain nobility. It was both enormous and colossal and yet remained a thing of grandeur. There was never a hint of vulgarity, or anything that reminded of the disordered, noisy coarseness of our democratic gatherings.

There was this same simplicity in the decoration of halls and auditoriums: red wall banners, on the bottoms of which stood out in silvered relief, swastikas alternating with eagles, no longer the bicephalic eagle of the defunct empire, but the quasi-roman eagle of the Holy Roman-Germanic Empire: the emblem of the revolution side by side with that of the monarchy. What more eloquent symbol of the perenniality of empire and of race! The Germans jealously retain the slightest relics of their national traditions: the eagle of Barbarossa[7] nestled with the gamutted cross of Hitler. We French on the other hand, have thrown our fleurs de lys by the wayside.

There was a profusion of flags and banners everywhere: in windows, down each street, on public

---

[7] Translator's Note: the eagle of Barbarossa pertains to the Empire of Frederick I, by-named Frederick Barbarossa ("Redbeard") 1123-1190, a German king who struggled for predominance over other European monarchies and steadfastly opposed the authority of the Popes. Not to be confused with Kahyr Ad-din, the Ottoman "redbeard" of the 16th century.

monuments, and along the highways. One might even say there were too many. An orgy of red flags which completely overwhelmed those of the social-democrats. So! You want red flags Mr. Socialist and Mr. Communist? We'll give them to you! You shall be drowned in red; you shall be engulfed to the point of making your head swim!... All the while, it is necessary to acknowledge that the organizers of these rallies knew how to obtain extraordinarily decorative effects from the massing of these flags. In this vein, the most astonishing sight which I contemplated occurred Friday, September 13th, on the Zeppelinwiese, an event featuring a processional march with 20,000 banners, representing National Socialist groups form every city and province in Germany. The Zeppelinwiese stadium is immense, able to hold spectators numbering in the hundreds of thousands. This particular day it was full, to the point where the compressed mass of participants became oddly indistinguishable from the neighboring terrain, giving the impression of a cultivated field ploughed as far as the eye could see, where the human columns seemed as furrows traced by a plow[8]. In the center of this giant field, covered entirely by soldiers in arms, existed an avenue large as the bed of a river, which extended to the distant horizon... Suddenly, an imperceptible Wagnerian orchestra filled the air with triumphal sound: the March of the Niebelungen.... And then from the far end of the assembly, at the very

[8] Translator's Note: this calls to mind the immortal scene from Leni Rieffenstahl's "Triumph des Willens," shot from behind the podium, in the spectator's stand, the same view Bertrand is describing.

extremity of the avenue which leads up to the Führer's rostrum, a dark reddish mass raised up like that which proceeds the sun in the morning sky. It was the approach of those 20,000 banners, shuddering towards us. In rhythm with the triumphal music, the massive columns came forth, stretching out into a vast expanse of red, suddenly stopping in one single motion. Then, with another single motion, the 20,000 banners were raised, appearing like great reddish bouquets, then lowered in an unanimous salute before the diminutive brown-shirted figure, barely discernible at the podium above, he who represented the master of the Third Reich....

This slender brown figure, I again saw him the following day, descended from the podium at the stadium parade field, attending another pass-and-review, this time of regimented workers. This pass-and-review, impressive both in numbers and in discipline, lasted several hours. The Führer was there, standing in his car, immobile, indefatigable, with arm outstretched saluting that army of workers who represented, on this day, Germany in arms. And this diminutive man, with his arm raised in salutation, a gesture having the appearance of sovereignty, this humble man, without crown, without scepter sewn with golden bees, nor baton of rulership, evoked the image of the imperial figure from "La Distribution des Aigles..."[9]

---

[9] Translator's Note: trans. "The Distribution of Eagles": the referenced event is unknown.

What struck me most during the course of these militarist demonstrations was the pacific character they seemed to observe, as if by specific intent. Neither from the crowds of people, nor from the hundreds of thousands of men in arms, inflamed by the most vehement nationalistic oratory, did I ever once hear a war cry or a hateful expression against anyone - not even against the Jews. And what astonished me even more, I who passed a part of my youth in Alsace-Lorraine and remember the haughty arrogance of the German officers in the streets of Metz and Strasbourg, was the disappearance, in this new army, of the type of country squire attitudes and behavior found previously. To a great extent, this army of the masses had become democratized. Is it the army or the civilian that has disappeared? One can no longer be sure. Everyone appears to be in uniform and boots. During these days of festivity, a singular bourgeois merriment seemed to combine both ranks and classes. The beer gardens and restaurants were full of persons seated at table consuming liters of beer and gorging themselves on sausages. One would say even this overindulgence itself was regulated. There was no fighting or brawling, no shouting or discordant gestures. This otherwise well-mannered crowd became animated only when someone announced the approach of the Führer. At this, everyone would suddenly get up, pressing one another to see and cheer him.

And he was everywhere. He showed himself freely, standing or seated in his uncovered automobile. He was incessantly in contact with the popular masses.

And not only did he respond to their ovations, he spoke to them and harangued them every day, several times a day, even. There was no event or gathering where Hitler did not speak…

When he appeared, followed by his retinue, either in the open air or within the confines of a meeting hall, I noticed in his grim face a nervous contraction that pulled the edges of his lips, and at the same time, a haggard and menacing expression in his gaze: it was perhaps the "on-guard" of the combatant who enters the arena and who, abruptly, finds himself face to face with wild animals - or the instinctive reaction of a hunted man who might at any moment expect a bomb or a bullet. But this lasted for only a few seconds at most. Soon his face relaxed and he even began to smile in recognition of friends or persons he knew. In passing, he gave a friendly wave or a slight nod. One had the impression he was a man of resolve, someone who goes straight for his goal, without fear, without hesitation - a very courageous and unprepossessing person. Above all, it was his simplicity that was most striking. Firstly, in his dress: bare head and in uniform, like a soldier of the Party, wearing boots, tunic, and a soft collar with a sailor-knot tie. Then again, he had a simplicity in his gait and mannerisms. By contrast, I think of other dictators. Regarding this diminutive worker who was going to speak in the name of Germany before 300,000 listeners, there was not the slightest shade of pretension or pompous behavior.

There he was before the microphone. Same simplicity in his use of language as in his mannerisms. People have spoken to me with praise about his eloquence, and described him as a great orator. I hesitate to offer a hasty opinion. Although I was very near to him, his voice came back distorted due to the loud speakers. It appeared both rough and hollow. But perhaps it is the German language that produced this effect on me. In any case, I noted a clear disdain for oratorical artifice. His gestures were modest, almost non-existent. Hitler spoke, his two hands crossed over his chest, like a preacher in the pulpit. He spoke a long time, a very long time, to the point where I was astonished at the patience and the religious silence of that innumerable audience. He made them no concession of flattery or vulgarity. He spoke of things both serious and substantial, which he succeeded in impressing upon his audience through a combination of obstinacy and faith. And then, of a sudden, he became heated and cried out in the manner of a mass orator - unleashing a chain reaction of wild enthusiasm throughout the entire stadium, with long, surging applause and thunderous cheering, lacking perhaps the spontaneity and individual note we are used to in France. What it lacked in this manner of expression was made up for by the sheer intensity of acclamation.

Here he was, therefore, in his primary endeavor, this man who dared assume the demanding task of leading an entire people. How are we to understand such ascendancy over the masses? Those people who have an answer for everything say that he has "the charm" or "the fluid." I didn't feel Hitler had one or the other. I merely attest to the fact he pleases: and there you have it. He pleases by his extreme simplicity, by a total absence of posturing, a spirit of camaraderie, and without a doubt, also by an untamed energy marking his appearance and which distinguishes him as a leader as well as a man who came from the ranks. The born leader, from wherever he comes, from whatever low station he issues, is never a vulgar individual. Hitler came from a lower middle-class background, rubbing shoulders with the working-class: one sees this. But one also sees in him the type of distinction appropriate to someone in command. This mark of distinction Hitler possesses to the highest degree. As I said however, he even has something of a common distinction. I watched him come forth, greet and discourse with those around him, or, quite simply, just listen. At one point, a prince of the royal family passed by. If I hadn't known who he was, I would readily have guessed which of the two was dictator: I would have hesitated in choosing the prince.

At first glance, the Führer had a rather ordinary appearance. But once he advanced to the edge of the stage in order to speak, or was standing in his automobile to salute the crowd, or the Reich's militia,[10] he suddenly became a different man: "surrounded by blazing eyes fixed on him," he was transfigured. Before the Germany that acclaimed him, he became Germany

---

[10] Translator's Note: in speaking of the "Reich's militia," the author is likely referring to the Sturmabteilungen, the brown-shirted S.A.

itself: he revealed in turn its own transfigured and magnificent image. It was no longer he who one saw, it was sixty-five million people overwhelmed by the joy of being reborn, prey to the delirium of grandeur and acclaiming themselves in this person.

We several Frenchmen were there watching, our hearts burdened yet overwhelmed by the beauty of such a spectacle. We were asking ourselves, "Why don't we see anything like this back home?… These multitudes, this discipline, this unanimity that above all gives the impression of invincible force!…"

II

How One Becomes A Dictator

In order to explain, to a certain degree, the paradoxical fortune of Hitler, it is necessary to understand the state of Germany following the armistice.

Generally speaking, the close of World War I found Germany in disarray, its public affairs in ruins. There was widespread famine and general misery. The army no longer existed. In the midst of these misfortunes came the menace of separatism, foreign agitation, and the imminent dislocation of the Empire.[1] There existed

[1] Translator's Note: the provisions of the Treaty of Versailles, which went into effect 10 January 1920, turned over all Germany's colonies in China and the Pacific north of the equator to Japan, while Britain accrued all possessions in the Pacific south of the equator, as well as in East and Southwest Africa, France receiving territories in West Africa north of the Congo.

a general anarchy of central authority, in contrast with the various intrigues of numerous secret associations.

The most humiliating factor for this proud nation, well used to considering itself foremost in Europe, was the presence of the victor. And among the occupation forces, those most difficult to accept in the opinion of the Germans were our black soldiers. It is quite evident that Germany does everything it can to discredit our colonial auxiliaries, just as it has never ceased to defame our Foreign Legion, because these contingents constitute a considerable reinforcement to our defense. But it is quite certain also - let us say this in passing - that it was a mistake on our part to have the vanquished guarded by blacks and Asians. Were we so exhausted at this point that it was necessary for us to fall back on men of color to replace our own soldiers? Or rather were we wanting to inflict this supreme humiliation on a people so intensely racist by having them guarded and held in abeyance by races they considered inferior?

During this difficult period, which appeared seemingly hopeless, there were no men of State, no champions or saviors leading the way to recovery. Hitler, who experienced this debacle, sensed the approach of ultimate defeat for Pan Germanism. In Austria, a country made up of bits and pieces, he had been able to assess the danger of racial chaos. For him, there was no shadow of doubt. Among all these various competing nationalities, it was Germany that should be the leader, by virtue of being the most dynamic, the most intelligent and the greatest organizer. At all cost, it was necessary to save what was German. Meanwhile in France, we were astonished that it was an Austrian who had assumed this task. For we considered Hitler a foreigner relative to Germany, forgetting that Austria had always been part of Germany, and for centuries the seat of the Germanic Holy Roman Empire.[2] Above all, we forget that nationalism is more revered by men of the borderlands than by those of the interior. I have listened to Belgian Walloons proclaim themselves more French than the Frenchmen of France and recall that Joan of Arc came form the borders of Lorraine.

Faced with the German collapse, what might have been the reaction of a former soldier like Hitler, a proletarian who had seen the world of the laborer up close and at the same time, was a nationalist and ardent Germanophile?

The urgent task that pressed upon his senses was to oppose separatism by every means, and more generally, everything of an international nature; consequently, to oppose Marxism, the most active form of internationalism. After this, it would be necessary to reunify and bring cohesion to the Reich, restoring its liberty and its rank as a great European nation, and, in order to reach this goal, to evade or reject the most subjugating clauses of the Versailles Treaty.

---

[2] Translator's Note: the Hapsburg Dynasty began with Rudolf I in 1273 and lasted intermittently until Francis II's renunciation of "Holy Roman Emperor" to become Emperor Francis I of Austria in 1806.

In order to accomplish these things, a leader is needed. At the outset, it is doubtful whether Hitler saw himself as this person. A leader only discovers himself little by little. It is necessary for him to experience the trial of circumstances and be graced with a degree of favorable chance. But what Hitler understood from the outset was the necessity to create a party that opposed separatism, as well as one that stood against internationalism and the strict abeyance of treaties. He had the good fortune to find such a party already existing in embryonic state. In effect, this party existed in Munich after the war,[3] a "German Workers' Party" to which he hastened to affiliate himself.[4] This party did not yet contain but a very small membership. The question was how to develop it to the point where it would become a great national party, capable of displacing Marxism? Where to find allies? Hitler and his colleagues resolutely separated themselves from social democracy. On the other hand, they perceived the former imperial government was no longer possible. Notwithstanding, they were obliged to admit the previous regime contained some good elements. If they reproved its diplomacy and

---

[3] Translator's Note: Anton Drexler, together with Rudolf Freiherr von Sebottendorff (leader of the Thule Society), and Karl Harrer, organized the first meeting of the German Workers' Party in January 1919. Hitler's first introduction to this party occured on September 12 of the same year.

[4] Translator's Note: according to American historian John Toland, after attending two meetings, Hitler was still undecided. Dismayed by the lack of practical organization but attracted by the personal opportunity for politics, joining the GWP was the "hardest question" of his life.

alliances, they admired its stable government, due to the presence and action of an individual leader. They envied its army and powerful organizational structure. The eventual goal was to rebuild this army, to solidify centralized authority through administrative echelons, and ultimately to reduce parliament to its consultative role, while reinforcing the authority and powers of the Chief of State.

Who can be depended on to carry out the National Socialist program? The intellectuals were out of the question. A party directed by gentlemen of letters is devoted to powerlessness. The action of a great writer or a great thinker is much more restricted than one would imagine. In order to be effective, this action needs to pass into more energetic hands than those of an intellectual. It is not enough to think correctly in order to have an influence on politics. Without risk of paradox, one might even attest that such correctness of thought is an obstacle to its dissemination: the latter must instead falsify to a certain extent, to affect the masses, who trouble themselves very little about rational thinking. To attain power, intellectuals are bad companions. It is necessary to instead have the complicity of the masses. Yet when Hitler affiliated himself with the German Worker's Party, the masses were almost totally controlled by the Marxist Social-Democrats. Reversing this trend was therefore a quite formidable undertaking.

The only effective method was to make direct contact with the masses, to speak with and to show them, in the guise of a true leader, a brighter future and a more rewarding material life. What is important here is to act through the spoken word and to acquire popularity by addressing those words directly to the people. I don't know if Hitler has perfected the art of eloquence, or if he has added anything to the practice or technique of public gatherings. But in any case, he is truly a popular speaker and has rigorously applied the rules of the public gathering. He is convinced what one says in these gatherings has only a secondary importance. The important thing is the manner of saying it. The principal task is to motivate. And one can only motivate crowds by delusions of vengeance, of better-being, of material satisfaction, or by over-exciting racial instinct or national pride. No interruptions can be tolerated. The party speaker must be allowed to speak; absolute liberty for him but none for the adversary. This liberty must extend even to street demonstrations: it must be held firmly in the hands of the party. Counter demonstrators, like those who would interrupt meetings, are to be treated with the utmost violence.

We recognize here the methods employed for quite some time by the Socialists and Communists. Hitler has merely responded to terror with terror. Those who reproach his methods should equally reproach those who gave him the example. In any event, from the outset, he employed them with marvelous audacity and supreme energy.

In 1922, in the city of Coburg, Hitler arranged to celebrate "German Day." Communist and Marxist labor unions tried to stop this gathering. He ignored the many threats, descending from the train with 800 men, and, with musicians at the lead, amid the hoots and insults of the opposition, proceeded down the streets of the city. It was not long before coming to blows. But after fifteen minutes of fighting, the Reds were dispersed. On the following day, they ineffectively tried to stop the departing column of Hitlerians returning to the train station. Not able to do this, they finally wanted to impede the train's departure. But among his men, Hitler had mechanics who could take over if necessary. Not only did he order them to replace the Red mechanics, but, preparing for an attempt en route, he announced he was going to choose Communist leaders as hostages to share the dangers of the voyage. This sufficed to calm the passing fancy of resistance. The train departed, arriving without hindrance in Munich.

In the wake of their demonstrations and gatherings, the National Socialists gained publicity by word of mouth, and above all, through the press. But as was cynically stated by the silent partner of one of our large dailies: "A newspaper is a business," and a press is therefore not unbiased. A newspaper is always in the service of someone or something. Therefore, German National Socialism needed to have one for itself. And this all the more because the German press was, to a large extent, in the hands of the Jews, and in consequence, indentured to Marxism. The activity of the press by itself is ineffectual if one does not succeed in overcoming the enemy's organizations. Those of the Social Democrats were extraordinarily powerful. The only means of destroying them was to secretly infiltrate their ranks and create disunity to the point where they were ultimately defeated. Similarly for Parliamentarianism. The Hiterian party struggled to gain access into parliament up to the day when it was able to overthrow and suppress it. This was no longer a new idea. And it is still the tactic employed by our Socialists and Communists. But the means count for nothing. Success depends uniquely on the leader.

The leader! It is not necessary that he be a genius. What he needs is energy, perseverance, and above all, audacity. He must not be reluctant to defend himself. A leader, like a regime, who no longer knows how to defend himself, is lost. And it is not enough merely to defend, but to strike as well. A leader must know how to attack, to instill fear and confusion among the ranks of the enemy. A certain coarseness coupled with prompt decision-making is also necessary. He must avoid the ineffectual behavior of intellectuals and men of letters who do not know how to seize the occasion, who are stymied by a multitude of scruples, who forever hesitate, because at bottom, they are horrified by action. If the leader wishes to know great popularity, he must be energetic and decisive, but he must also be selfless. He shall be an example of absolute dedication to the public weal. Everyone will know he has dedicated his life, that he is ready to sacrifice it for the benefit of the State... Undoubtedly, one will also know he depends on all sorts of friendships, or "filiations" as was said in the republics of antiquity, of which he has amazing good fortune, not to mention a large number of more or less obscure collaborators. But one shall also know he is of one will and that, whatever influences he encounters, he has the firm intent to govern by his own thinking, to direct events and master the situation to the greatest degree possible by a single human will.

Hitler inspects Hitler Youth. Max Amman to Hitler's left. Courtesy Library of Congress.

Hitler Youth at Nuremberg. Courtesy Library of Congress.

**The Sturmabteilung (SA) pass in review.
Courtesy Library of Congress.**

The Sturmabteilung (SA) march through the streets of Nuremberg. Courtesy Library of Congress.

III

Ideology of the National Socialist Party

In the same way we have considered only the principle stages and essential politics of Hitler's rise to power, similarly, as to the party's ideology, we will consider only the truly representative ideas, those that have entered into practice and seem to have a place in the future. A number of accessory ideas appear to have already been abandoned, or put on hold for a more appropriate time.

By 1920, the National German Worker's Party had an established program that it proclaimed during the course of a mass rally that same year in Munich.[1] Since then, the Party has been calling for Germany's equality of rights with other nations: it is this "gleichberichtigung" about which we in France

[1] Translator's Note: Bertrand is referring to 24 February 1920 at Munich's famous Hofbrauhaus.

have made such a fuss recently. When emotions will have calmed, we shall no longer understand why this issue caused such an uproar. There is one of two things here: either a nation is enslaved and the question of its rights is irrelevant, or it is a free nation with the same rights as all others. It is your choice to either reduce that nation to total subjugation or to take measures that comport the liberty you have granted. When we fail to choose either option, our recriminations make us look ridiculous.

Since 1920, the German Worker's Party has demanded the abolition of the Treaties of Versailles and Saint-Germain. It calls for the restitution of former German colonies, or at least the right to acquire new ones. Along with this, it puts forth the principle of extensive nationalization: civil rights curtailed for non-Germans, freedom of the press and general liberties allowed only to those of the German race; abolition of all revenues not earned from work; participation by workers in the profits of the enterprise; the press under the control of the State; liberty of conscience, and liberty for any denomination on condition they do not militate against the German national sentiment; recognition of the right of private property, but only to a certain point: intensive and abusive capitalization runs counter to the authority and liberty of the State; nationalization of existing industrial combines and financial houses. The State should be in control of the banks; all indigenous Germans shall have a right to a viable pension, starting at a given age, or in the case of injury. Finally, the German Worker's Party also calls for the creation of a professional army and the return to obligatory military service. Along with this is the struggle against Marxism, and against the Jews who sustain it.[2]

It is perhaps unnecessary to mention that the foregoing program was not fully implemented. What remains unshakable, however, is the will to achieve national rejuvenation and give satisfaction to the aspirations of the proletariat; the latter being subordinate to the former. But above all, what is essential to the program is the belief that the will, the German will, can achieve whatever it desires. In 1934, at Nuremberg, the central theme of the Reichsparteitag was: "Triumph of the Will."[3] This is a worthy lesson for peoples whose will has become enfeebled. Already by the end of the last century, Nietzsche classified peoples by the degree of their national will: the Germans came first, followed by, surprisingly, the Russians, then the Corsicans and the Spanish. We French were at the low end of the scale. In any case, this faith in the omnipotence of the will is something profoundly German. The cult of action proclaimed by Goethe is basically the cult of the will. And it is again the will that is the basis of

---

[2] Translator's Note: for a fuller treatment of the Twenty-five Point Thesis, from which this derives, see Michael Oakeshott, "The Social and Political Doctrines of Contemporary Europe," Cambridge University Press, London, 1941, pp. 190–193.

[3] Translator's Note: the reader will recognize this as the name adopted by the 1934 documentary "Triumph des Willens," filmed and directed by Leni Riefenstahl.

Schopenhauer's philosophy - the will, a distinct reality, a primary reality, while the intellect is only secondary.

It can be seen that the German will to resurgence profoundly differs from our French idea of "Revanche,"[4] as much as Hitlerism differs from "déroulédisme."[5] For us, it is simply a question of beating the enemy after he has beaten us: a question of means and of armaments. For Hitler, it is a question of remaking an entire nation from top to bottom. This is not only the "intellectual and moral reform" that Renan[6] asked for following our national disaster,[7] it is also a social and political reform - a totalitarian reform that is, in reality, a significant national revolution.

To reshape the nation with greater strength than it has ever possessed: here is the problem.

Yet the nation is encircled by enemies - enemies from without and within. The latter are the most dangerous, and, among these, the most dangerous of all are the international Marxists, because they know how to address the masses and possess formidable means of action and propaganda. I speak of Marxism

---

[4] Translator's Note: a term popularized after the French defeat of 1870, meaning "revenge."

[5] Translator's Note: A coined word based on the more formal "déroulement": unrolling, unfolding, hence, to allow events to take place in due course.

[6] Translator's Note: Auguste Renan (1823 - 1892) French scholar, historian and philosopher of religion.

[7] Translator's Note: i.e., the disaster of the Franco-Prussian War of 1870.

at the service of international finance, working for this international finance while destroying the economies of all nations.

In the guise of working for the liberation of the universal proletariat, in reality, Marxism is only working for a single nation, or then again, a single dominant race. And in the guise of defending the universal proletariat, in reality, it only seeks to defend the manual worker: concerning itself only with those of the city, where it likewise savagely undermines intellectual and moral values. It is no longer Socialism, but rather class tyranny. This humane society no longer aims to include all men. It instead establishes, to the benefit of the most inferior humanity, a regime of casts. This is a reversal of natural order, an ignorant defiance of both reason and justice.

In all nations to which it is introduced, Marxism is an instrument of division and national decline. And, in this regard, one cannot help noticing that it admirably serves the age-old and millennial tactic of Israel, which consists of weakening its adversaries and dividing them in order to better insure its reign. This explains the deliberately hostile attitude taken by German public opinion against both the Jews and against Marxism, that doctrine of Jewish origin considered as a secret means of domination in the hands of international Jewish finance. And here we are brought to the burning question that Germany assumes to definitively resolve by radical methods: that of racism and anti-Semitism.

Let us readily say that it is difficult for outsiders to allow themselves to understand the reasons that caused Hitlerism to adopt such broad and rigorous methods. We do not understand that an entire people or race be made responsible for the misdeeds of some, or that a minority be chastised for the wrong-doing or dangerous tendencies of the majority. We presume that special protective or surveillance measures would suffice for preventing a category of citizens from forming a State within a State. Seen from the outside, German anti-Semitism appears to be a gross iniquity.

Given this reservation, let us see how the question stands with the Germans.

The Germans realize we spew hostile criticism against their racism. All the while, no one even dreams of denouncing American racism, Hindu racism, or that of the Chinese or Japanese that we can also describe as prejudice for or against the races of color. And yet all races have the right to defend themselves, especially the superior races, although there are those among them, perhaps even a majority, whose capacity for civilization seems given over to a perpetual inferiority.

Let us add that race is not - as Gobineau[8] offered all too readily - something primarily physiological, but a complexity of aptitudes, or moral-intellectual tendencies, more or less influenced by nurture or

---

[8] Translator's Note: Arthur de Gobineau (1816-1882), French diplomat and ethnologist.

heredity. In the final analysis, Gobineau wasn't far from seeing in race the presence of a metaphysical entity that occurs independently from heredity or environmental conditions. However it be, for the most part Israel was and still is a nation of racial intransigence that does not allow itself to mix with outsiders, else allows it only to more surely and completely dominate the race with which it allies itself. The transmission of certain physiological qualities is only a secondary matter. It is more essential to impose a certain character and mentality. It has been humorously said that every young Jew is born with a university professorship. More certain is that they have the presumption to be the world's teachers. The Jew's primary contention seems to be: "How can an intelligent man such as you not think like me?"

One can proceed to explain the attitude of German racism in regard to Israel. It is a case of two equally intransigent racisms that confront each other. Aside from this, Hitler and his followers cannot overlook the fact that all their enemies - Social Democrats, Communists, and Bolsheviks - count a large number of Jews in their ranks. There wasn't but a single step between this fact and the accusation that all such revolutionary parties are inspired, supported, and lead by Jews. What is more, the Hitler movement couldn't fail to realize that the Jew, destroyer of foreign nations, had never been able to found a nation of their own and is absolutely void of political spirit, while all the while aspiring to control universal politics. Such an imperialism is the natural ally of Bolshevist imperialism, if it isn't already part of the same fabric to begin with.

For the Germans, such are the reasons that justify their anti-Semitism. In sum, their fight against the Jew is an effort to defeat Bolshevism.[9]

When the Germans say they have no greater enemy - that Europe has no greater enemy - than Bolshevism, I am certain they are absolutely sincere. And, when they maintain that their National Socialism has saved Europe from a Bolshevik insurrection, they scarcely exaggerate.

In his most recent speech, Adolf Hitler thoroughly expounded what National-Socialism opposes about Bolshevism. It is worth emphasizing and clearly underlining his exact thoughts, because they are constantly misrepresented by our press and because here in France, it is a common form of argument to declare that Hitlerism and Bolshevism resemble each other so closely as to be easily confused:

"National Socialism", says Hitler, "is a doctrine which exclusively concerns the German people. Bolshevism by contrast, proclaims an international mission… Bolshevism preaches universal class

---

[9] Translator's Note: in reading *Mein Kampf*, or Hitler's speeches (see Norman F. Bains: *The Speeches of Adolf Hitler*), it is clear the fight against the Jew is much more than the defeat of Bolshevism.

struggle, international and world revolution, by a process of terror and violence.

"National Socialism fights for a logical conciliation and resolution of fundamental antagonisms and for the consolidation of the German people for the purpose of achieving common goals…

"National Socialism attributes no value to the theoretical supremacy of the working class. By contrast, it attributes much greater value to the practical improvement of living conditions and the general welfare of this class…[10]

"As National Socialists, we are filled with admiration and reverence for the great achievement of the past, not only for those that sprang from our own people, but those that came from outside our borders. We are pleased to belong to a community of European culture that has, to such a large degree, stamped the present world with the imprint of its spirit.

"Bolshevism rejects this cultural past and affirms that the history of civilization and humanity only began with the birth of Marxism.

---

[10] Translator's Note: Guy Sajer's *The Forgotten Soldier* details the reaction of the average German soldier on the Eastern Front when encountering the squalid living conditions of the Russian working class by comparison with their own conditions of life under Nazism.

"As National Socialists, we consider private property to correspond with a superior phase of economic development… that, on the whole, makes possible and guarantees to all a higher standard of living."

In this manner does Hitler solemnly condemn Bolshevism's essential principles. He especially condemns the idea of class struggle, an idea both hideous and cannibalistic that Marxism has spread throughout the world, finding cause with the most barbaric xenophobes. In sum, Hitler declares that for a people as long civilized as the Germans, subscribing to the principles of Bolshevism would equate to a shameful digression and a veritable degradation. For Bolshevism is the great enemy, not only of every German, but of all civilized peoples.

The nationalization toward which Hitlerism seems headed is indisputably opposed to the French and Latin idea of individualism. Hitler acknowledges this and explains that he is forced to this extreme nationalization by the circumstances and necessities of his struggle. Similarly, he expresses concern over the need for "autarchy," and the state of isolation and economic defense to which Europeans see themselves constrained. Yet this, he feels, is a passing stage. In any case, the fiercely nationalist and authoritarian regime to which Germany believes it must submit implies no hostility in regard to its neighbor-nations.

In that which concerns France, Hitler has repeated in a lengthy discourse before the Reichstag last spring that he has the most ardent desire to reach a mutual understanding and that, with the Saar affair now settled, he renounces any further territorial claims. In general, the tone of this discourse couldn't have been more peace-minded or conciliatory and, I might even add, "democratic" in the same sense we would understand. To any observer of good will, one would say that things have certainly changed since the time of William II.

One feels, in each of these declarations, a great desire to defuse animosity, to heal old wounds and to reassure Europe of intentions that might otherwise appear bellicose. To those who reproach his policy of rearmament and the breaking of treaties, the Chancellor replies - and it's his main argument - that the Allies gave him an example of all of this by being the first to break the Treaty of Versailles in refusing to disarm - and he denounces above all the massive armaments of the Russians: "It is inadmissible," he concludes, "that one State body presents its armaments as an olive branch of peace and those of others as the pitchfork of the devil…"

We needn't ask ourselves what lies behind these continual peace overtures. They may be perfectly sincere: they even give this impression. But despite all, it also remains clear that Germany under Hitler, no more than under William II, has not renounced the salutary cult of force; whether one calls this dynamism, will, or force, it's all the same thing.

Our neighbors are always thinking along the same lines. They think one must always expect to be attacked. If you do not attack, you will be attacked. If you do not wish to be destroyed, you must prevent the enemy by being ten times stronger. Don't deceive yourself with the illusion that you can live without worry, at peace with all your neighbors. Of course, you wish to relax and enjoy your acquired fortune. You tell yourself you no longer have any desire for gain or for conquest. You are satisfied and content. But the neighbor is not. He has no desire to relax. You cannot just cross your arms, for if you do you will be overrun by those who are aggressive, by those who consider action as the very sign of life, and war as the natural condition of humanity.

Don't say this is a condition of barbarism, a stage long past. The nations that surround you are still in this state of affairs. Look at the mess in the Balkans! And what about this "dynamism" which certain countries proclaim? Russia is "dynamic." Italy also, and Japan even moreso still. Why shouldn't Germany be "dynamic" like all peoples who look forward to a great and glorious future? Just as there will always be the poor and undernourished, there shall always be those who are aggressive. The rule of morality can only attenuate the methods of aggression but not suppress the aggressive instinct.

And so here is how the Reich has put itself back on a war footing and how it has rebuilt its army of former times. It pretends not to want to attack anyone: it insists only on making itself respected, and defending a liberty dearly re-conquered. But it is always necessary to expect an attack at one's borders and to prevent this, if possible. Here is the crux of Hitlerism: to defend German Liberty. Only just last year at Nuremberg, the party's watch-word was: "Liberty." No doubt this liberty is worrisome for all of Germany's neighbors. Rest assured she will not hesitate to invoke it the moment one of her vital interests, or the certainty of victory, suggests itself.

IV

What Might Our Attitude Be Toward Hitlerism

At present, there is a prevailing attitude represented by most of the press and French opinion at large, but which is based on foolishness, lack of understanding, and fear. It is an attitude of peevishness, jealousy, chicanery, and absurd prejudice that denies all evidence and refuses to see things as they really are. Quite recently a German statesman was telling me, not without a bit of roguish irony: "How very strange! You are the victors and yet, it is you who bear us a grudge!..." It is evident we are not very chivalrous. But perhaps we have good reason for this - reasons that our neighbor too easily forgets: our land invaded, millions of dead, our people decimated, unprecedented destruction and atrocities, and finally, the flagrant intent to humiliate and cripple us forever: of all the injuries to which we were subjected, it is perhaps this one we found the most bitter and unforgettable.

To this the Germans respond with the number of their dead, the billions in imposed reparations, the suffering during the blockade and ensuing famine, the ten year occupation of a part of their territory: given these humiliations in contrast with ours, they say we have nothing to envy. And when we reproach them with responsibility for the war, they hold us no less accountable. Who will decide between us? It is quite certain we never wanted this war. Yet could we ever have refused once it was imposed on us? We remain firm in our point of view. But the Germans remain no less firm in theirs. Despite our protests, they claim our alliances, although purely defensive according to us, were a threat to them given that our allies either induced or obliged us to mobilize (a claim confirmed by circumstance), given above all, our total refusal to undertake friendly relations with them since 1870, our animosity flamed by our defeat, and, in the name of immanent justice, our secret desire for a favorable circumstance that would permit us to retake our possessions without drawing swords. Here is therefore what the Germans think: they are convinced the responsibilities for the war must be shared by each of the belligerents.

Not only do we bear the Germans a grudge for declaring war against us, but for our own inability to sufficiently defeat them afterwards. We bear them this same grudge for their rapid recovery, which we have not known how or been able to impede. And finally, we resent their tearing up treaties, despite they were imposed by force. This is what we call their "bad faith" (Ah! - didn't we similarly tear up the Treaty of Frankfurt?). But having done this they regained the ranks of a free people and again became a great military power. Instead of viewing this fact with the seriousness it deserves and conducting our actions accordingly, we give ourselves over to idle blustering. We refuse to even enter into simple conversation with our old enemy out of who knows what silly fear for their treachery. But as it is an excellent means of assuring our security, we count on our other neighbors to do this for us. We sign pacts with Peter and Paul, and no doubt we shall soon sign them with the entire world, without really knowing what guarantees they offer. With all due seriousness we read in the papers that a coalition of peace-minded people will surely know how to make Germany remain docile. But where are these pacifist-minded persons? Would they be in Russia by any chance? I don't want to mention any country aside form this one. Nearly all Europe is a vast hornet's nest in a state of turmoil. In central Europe there isn't a single country that is content with its lot or feels secure from aggression. Therefore, from where do we speak of a coalition of peace-minded people? Is it possible to indulge in such nonsense!

All this lacks common sense. We can't continue to take a stiff-necked attitude with Germany as with people who don't want to know anything, or assume to shroud ourselves in dignity while engaging in a ridiculous mania for alliances. This is much more incomprehensible than the Germans themselves, the defeated of yesterday, who take the first steps by offering us their hand. In our most basic interest, in the interest of the peace of Europe, we cannot afford to avoid these advances much longer. Before too long, it will be necessary to say "yes" or "no."

What do we say: "no?" That is fine by me. But let's take a look at the consequences.

Are we ready to again engage in an absurd and debilitating struggle, a struggle that is an equal calamity for both adversaries? I don't want to say anything to offend my own country, which it does not deserve. I am fully convinced that France is still capable of great heroism and dedication in facing up to the most challenging situations. She proved this many times during the course of the last war. And it is also certain that France is disposed of resources possibly unsuspected by our adversary, in terms of men and finance. Thanks to our colonial empire, we are re-establishing numerical equality with this enemy, even outdoing him to a large degree in the economic arena. However, all these advantages are nullified by the discouraging order of things which we have brought upon ourselves: waste, lack of foresight, disorganization, the slackening of our forces, and, above all, the demoralization of our nation. Let us consider only the apparent forces. I leave to our competent military authorities the responsibility for the numerical tallies which they draw up in their distressing studies I want to believe they exaggerate for the needs of the moment, so as to stimulate the blind inertia of our government. I am convinced that France still remains a military power of first order and that for anyone to try to subdue her would be a dangerous effort. But, alas, it is necessary to recognize that our governmental instability[1] and insufficient defensive preparations risk placing us, from the outset, in a state of inferiority. You will understand I am unable to say here all I am thinking, for such a subject is profoundly painful for a Frenchman.

According to our military writers, we are facing an army twice as large as our own and much better equipped. Can we at least count on our allies to make up the difference in numerical inequality? We have seen England's performance in 1914. She is certainly not a military power. All she had going for her was the prestige of her overseas empire and her naval force, factors that nevertheless would be juvenile to underestimate. With only England alone on our side, we came rather close to being defeated. Separated from us by the Alps, Italy has enough to do in defending her own borders. And let's be careful to realize that the situation is no longer

---

[1] Translator's Note: the threat of civil war forced the resignation of Premier Eduard Daladier in 1934. His successor, Gaston Doumergue, was replaced by Pierre Laval when the former's government disintegrated after the resignation of numerous radical ministers in 1935. Laval's sharp cuts in government spending and increased taxes to fight the Depression caused dissention within his Cabinet and became crucial election issues in the spring of 1936, elections that gave the Popular Front (a coalition of Communist and left-wing parties) a large majority in the Chamber of Deputies. The Socialists had by now become the largest party, with the Communists jumping from 10 to 72 seats. Léon Blum, a Jewish Socialist, became the new Premier. This, then, is the immediate background to Bertrand's remark.

the same as during the last war. The dispute between Italy and Ethiopia has recently embroiled us with our former allies, or at least dampened their sentiments in our regard. To what extent can we hope for their support? And this also takes into account that Italy, offended by our adherence to the Geneva sanctions, will not be reconciled by our differences with Germany.

After all this, can we seriously depend on the Petite Entente, which is composed of a considerable number of Germanic minorities and whose undefended territories it is to be feared will be invaded even before a declaration of war? What will Poland, Hungary, Austria, or Bulgaria do under these circumstances? It is very probable all these countries will align themselves on the side of Germany, above all if the latter's aggression against France automatically causes Russia to enter the fray. Yugoslavia remains doubtful. Yet it is above all the military value, the ability of these hybrid nations to defend themselves which remains uncertain. Regarding Russia, in her case as well, the efficacy of her intervention is extremely questionable, if only because of her distance from the German border. Even our most respected military leaders have formal reservations concerning this colossal Bolshevik army, about which we hear incessantly. Putting things at their best: let's assume the defeat of Germany and the triumph of a Franco-Russian-Balkan coalition. The consequence of this would be the complete bolshevization of Europe. Is this what you want?

I cannot understand how any civilized person would hesitate even an instant before giving an answer. No matter what, anything is better than being subjected to this type of regime and its consequent degradation!

To the contrary, in order to avoid the danger of an upheaval of this kind, with the abominable social repercussions that would follow, we should consent to speak with our neighbors outside the sainted halls of Geneva,[2] which is nothing more than an instrument of the occult, as one already knows; we should try to establish between us, if not relations of mutual trust, at least common interests we can both agree on. But first of all, this does not oblige us to break any of our existing friendships. England has sufficiently demonstrated its desire to reach agreement with Germany. For its part, Germany never misses an opportunity to similarly express desires to reach an understanding with England and France. Only a few months ago at Nuremburg, someone close to the Führer was telling me this was an intentional objective of German politics and that Germany would persevere to realize this goal. On the other hand, a settling of accounts as a means of being on friendlier terms with Germany in no way assumes that we are going to offer up our hearts and souls. We know all too well what separates us and that these essential differences are irreducible. We've already been studying each other such a long time now, examining each other in great detail, that any

[2] Translator's Note: it is to be recalled Geneva was home to the League of Nations.

surprise in this regard seems quite impossible. It is also understood that Germanic culture neither can, nor should, eliminate our own - and vice versa. During the discourse I mentioned earlier, Hitler was careful to say: "We are happy to belong to the community of European culture, a culture that has stamped the present world to such a large degree with its spirit." And as for Nazism itself, Hitler equally took care to affirm this: "National Socialism is a doctrine that exclusively concerns the German people. By contrast, Bolshevism proclaims it has an international mission..."

It is no longer a question of reducing ourselves to the role of "second place luminary," unless by pusillanimity or a desultory ignorance of our worth and all our resources - and an incomprehensible refusal to put them into effect - we accept this secondary role, something that would be more dangerous still. One of our diplomats of 1914 was telling me recently: "Be careful! If you cede the least little bit to Germany, you are going to find yourself in the same situation as Spain vis-a-vis France in the time of Napoleon. They will first ask for your neutrality, followed by certain endorsements, then monetary assistance, and finally your military cooperation. They will lead you into the worst adventures." This is perhaps evident only if we consider an accord with Germany as a soft pillow of security and idleness, or if we content ourselves with little or no active participation. An accord of equal footing can only mean complete parity, and can exist if we are resolved not only to use all our force, but to increase our strength as well. By no means can we just fold our arms. If we make a conscientious effort, let us make sure this effort is made in our best interests. It is the Germans themselves who exhort us, rather than offer our services to Europe and the world, to simply serve the interests of France.

For this, it is clear we need a national government and not a delegation from foreign shores.[3] It is further necessary that France remain resolutely France and not a disorderly assembly of Radical-Socialists or a criminal gang of Masonic-Bolsheviks.

Is there still time for France to reassert herself? Never before has the situation been more serious, for us as well as for the rest of Europe. Here we are, once again, threatened by war and on the verge of thralldom. What better time for our own sake to reflect upon the words of Rudolf Hess, one of the Führer's deputies, addressed not long ago to his fellow countrymen:

> "May the German people never forget what it means for a nation to have lost its liberty, and how difficult it is to reclaim it!..."

---

[3] Translator's Note: Louis Bertrand is obviously speaking of Léon Blum and his Socialist cabinet that took office following the spring elections of 1936.

Index

N

P

R

S

T

V

W

About the Translator

Dan Desjardins was born in Miami, Florida, 27 May 1954, the son of Ulysses John Joseph "Pete" Desjardins and Regine Madeleine Copus. Dan attended Williston Academy, an all-male prepatory school in Easthampton MA, followed by a freshman year at the American College in Paris. He attended Boston University, then Florida State, where he earned a bachelor's in Chemistry in 1977. As a commissioned officer with USAF, he earned a bachelor's in Electrical Engineering from the University of New Mexico in 1984. With a desire to pursue the Arts, he began an alternate career as playwright, achieving a Master's in Playwriting from Queen Margaret University College in Edinburgh. His full-length historical plays include *Der Anschluss* (1994) and *The Sudeten Crisis* (2000), and biographical plays *Lazarro Spallanzani* (1998) and *Marcus Aurelius* (2004). Dan is currently a Reserve Lieutenant Colonel with the United States Air Force. He is listed in *Who's Who In America* and is a member of Phi Alpha Theta historical society, Society for Information Displays and the International Society for Optical Engineering. He currently lives in North Carolina.

About the Author

Born at Spincourt, March 20, 1866, Louis Bertrand studied at Bar-le-Duc. He became a grammar-school teacher in Aix-La-Provence, later moving to Bourg-en-Bresse. In 1891, Monsieur Bertrand obtained a chair in Algeria, receiving a Doctor of Letters in 1897 with his thesis "The End of Classicism and the Return to Antiquity In the Second Half of the 18th Century and First Years of the 19th Century in France." He followed this in 1899 with his first book "The Blood of the Races," which treated the subject of heredity and the crossing of racial groups in Algeria. Bertrand's first novels appeared shortly thereafter, including "Don Juan's Rival" (1903) and "Pépète and Balthazar." In 1906 Bertrand traveled to the Orient, where he became passionately interested in questions of religion. After several accounts and novels based on his travels, including "Greece of Sun and Countryside" (1908) and "Mademoiselle from Jessincourt" (1911), he published "Saint Augustine" (1913), the first of his religious studies and one which classed him a master of artistic hagiography. During World War I, Bertrand wrote "Sanguis Martyrum," rallying fellow Frenchmen to the virtues of heroism. Following the war, in 1923, appeared "Louis XIV," followed by "Saint Teresa" (1924) and "Jean Perbal" in 1925. It was also in this year Louis Bertrand, recognized as one of France's foremost academicians, was elected to the Académie Française. "The New Sentimental Education" and "Hippolyte Porte-Couronnes" appeared in 1932. His later years were devoted to history: “History of Spain,” and works on Lorraine and Africa among these. His memoirs were contained in a series of novels under the title “d’Une Destinée,” of which 8 volumes appeared, to be followed by others, when he died on December 6, 1941, at Cap d’Antibes, North Africa.

Louis Bertrand. Courtesy Bettmann Archives.

www.ingramcontent.com/pod-product-compliance
Ingram Content Group UK Ltd.
Pitfield, Milton Keynes, MK11 3LW, UK
UKHW040019200726
13854UKWH00001B/267

9 781420 868012